TO:

May GOD'S BLESSINGS

fill your heart and life

FROM:

Requests for information should be addressed to:
Inspirio, the gift group of Zondervan
Grand Rapids, Michigan 49530
http://www.inspiriogifts.com

Associate Publisher: Tom Dean
Compiler: Doris Rikkers
Design Manager: Val Buick
Design: Lookout Design Group, Inc.

Printed in China
04 05 06/ HK/ 5 4 3 2 1

LIVING *Abundantly* THROUGH GOD'S BLESSING

JIM CYMBALA

inspirio™

CONTENTS

"I will send down

showers in season;

there will be showers

of blessing,"

says the Lord.

— EZEKIEL 34:26

THE HEART GOD BLESSES

Jesus said, "Blessed are
the pure in heart
for they will see God."
— Matthew 5:8

PREACHING FROM
THE HEART

One Sunday as I was in my office getting
ready for the afternoon service, I heard the
sound of people praying. The worship had just
begun, and the Prayer Band was already calling
on God. I distinctly heard a woman's voice say:
"God, protect him. Help him, Lord. Use him
to proclaim your Word today. Convict of sin;
change people, Lord!"

The church was packed as usual. The choir
sang, and I preached with all my heart about
the love of God. As I reached the end of my
message, I closed my eyes and urged people
to come to the front and respond to God's love.

A Jewish man about 25 years old, stood up
in the back row and began edging toward the
center aisle. He had a steel-gray 38-caliber
revolver in his right hand, leveled at me!
Down the aisle he came, the gun pointed right
at my chest.

Many in the congregation didn't notice
because their eyes, like mine, were closed.
The ones who saw him froze in terror. Even
the ushers seemed paralyzed. By the time they
sprang into action, it was too late — the man
was coming up the steps onto the platform.

All the while, I continued to implore the crowd to yield to God's love, having no idea that my life seemed in imminent danger.

Carol was playing the piano behind me. In panic she screamed my name, but I didn't hear her. Carol was sure she was about to witness the cold-blooded murder of her husband—and then what? Would the fellow turn on her next?

He did neither. Instead, he walked up right beside me and tossed the weapon onto the pulpit. I heard a crash, my eyes flew open—*and there's a gun on my pulpit!*

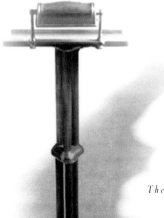

The man started to run back across the platform, down the steps, and up the aisle again. My only instinct was to chase after him and call, "No, no—don't go! It's okay. Wait!" He fell into a heap and began to weep as he cried out in a pitiful moan, "Jesus, help me! I can't take it anymore!"

By then the ushers were on top of him, not to harm him but to control the situation and to begin praying for him. Meanwhile, the church was in pandemonium. Some people were crying, others were praying aloud, still others sat in stunned silence.

In a moment I walked back up to the pulpit and I took a deep breath. I then held up the gun—not realizing it was loaded—and said, "Look what the love of God can make somebody give up."

Suddenly, from all over the building, people began to race to the altar. God had attached the final point to my message. A great harvest of needy souls came to the loving Christ that day.

As I watched the response, my mind went back to the woman's prayer a couple of hours earlier: "Lord, protect him today. Convict of sin; change lives. ..."

The man, somewhat unbalanced in his mind, said he had never intended to hurt me. He was planning to hurt somebody else … and he had just stopped by our meeting on the way. He became so convicted of the hate in his heart that he said to himself, *I have to get rid of this gun. I must give it to the preacher.*

As a result of the Prayer Band's praying straight into the face of danger, a life was spared. A great victory for God's kingdom was won; we baptized more than a dozen people as a result of that one meeting. The power of God's blessing was evident, and his work to change hearts went forward.

The Promise of Answered Prayer

GOD'S SEARCH

God is on a search.
He is not looking for such
things as knowledge or precious
stones—after all, he knows
everything and owns the world
and everything in it.
Although we rarely think about
this or hear it preached,
the Creator of all things is
looking throughout the whole
earth for a certain kind of heart.
He is searching for a human
heart that will allow him
to show how marvelously
he can strengthen, help, and
bless someone's life.

The eyes of the LORD range throughout
the earth to strengthen those whose hearts
are fully committed to him.

—2 CHRONICLES 16:9

The lamp of the LORD searches
the spirit of a man;
it searches out his inmost being.

—PROVERBS 20:27

Jesus said, "Suppose a woman has
ten silver coins and loses one. Does she
not light a lamp, sweep the house and search
carefully until she finds it? And when
she finds it, she calls her friends and neighbors
together and says, 'Rejoice with me;
I have found my lost coin.' In the same way,
I tell you, there is rejoicing in the presence
of the angels of God over one sinner
who repents."

—LUKE 15:8-10

The capital of heaven
is the heart in
which Jesus Christ
is enthroned as king.

—SADHU SUNDAR SINGH

GRANT ME, O GOD,
THE HEART OF A CHILD,
PURE AND TRANSPARENT AS A SPRING;
A SIMPLE HEART,
WHICH NEVER HARBORS SORROWS;
A HEART GLORIOUS IN SELF-GIVING,
TENDER IN COMPASSION;
A HEART FAITHFUL AND GENEROUS,
WHICH WILL NEVER FORGET ANY GOOD
OR BEAR A GRUDGE FOR ANY EVIL.

MAKE ME A HEART GENTLE AND HUMBLE,
LOVING WITHOUT ASKING ANY RETURN,
LARGE-HEARTED AND UNDAUNTABLE,
WHICH NO INGRATITUDE CAN SOUR
AND NO INDIFFERENCE CAN WEARY;
A HEART PENETRATED BY THE LOVE
OF JESUS
WHOSE DESIRE WILL ONLY BE SATISFIED
IN HEAVEN.

GRANT ME, O LORD,
THE MIND AND HEART
OF THY DEAR SON.

A French Prayer

CREATING A PURE HEART

In Psalm 51, King David asks God to "create in me a pure heart" (v. 10). David is asking for more than having his sin-stained heart washed. He is going deeper. What he desires is impossible for him; the Lord must do it. And the work must be done inside him. He wants God to start all over, to create a brand-new heart that is pure to the core. He admits that apart from God, he is all twisted inside. He wants to see everything in his world with pure eyes, to hear with holy ears, and to act with godly responses.

The word create here is the same one used in Genesis 1:1, when God created the heavens and the earth. It means a divine act of bringing something wonderful out of nothing. The work is all of God.

Let me say that receiving a pure heart from God is better than getting healed of cancer. It is better than becoming rich overnight. It is better than preaching marvelous sermons or writing best-selling books. Receiving a pure heart is to be like God at the core of your being.

The Sovereign Lord says: ... "I will give them an undivided heart and put a new spirit in them; I will remove from them their heart of stone and give them a heart of flesh. Then they will follow my decrees and be careful to keep my laws. They will be my people, and I will be their God."

—EZEKIEL 11:17, 19–20

If ... you seek the Lord your God, you will find him if you look for him with all your heart and with all your soul.

—DEUTERONOMY 4:29

THE MAN WITH A
HUMBLE HEART

I was about seven years old when an unusual man of God spoke at the midweek service of the small church my parents were attending. His name was Howard Goss, and I will never forget the impression he left on my young heart. Howard Goss didn't rant and rave to make his point. Nor did he use any emotional gimmicks as he delivered the Word of God. He simply explained the truths of Scripture in an easy conversational tone. But he also conveyed an unusual sense of the blessing of God.

I had been in the ministry for about six years when I visited the Philippines to speak at a large church. As I browsed in the pastor's study before the service, I noticed a book written by Howard Goss many years earlier. He had died since I had last seen him, but I still vividly remembered the impression he made on me.

The pastor noticed the book I was leafing through and abruptly exclaimed, "You know, his son goes to church here."

There was plenty of time before the service began, so I asked if I could meet him.

As we sat and talked, I explained my interest in knowing more about his dad. He told me about his father's conversion, long years of preaching ministry, and beautiful marriage. Then he opened up to me even more: "Even though I drifted away from God, I never could get away from my parents' prayers," he told me. "The farther I strayed, the more they interceded for me. Dad was always seeking God. I would so often see him on his knees in his study. His heart was so sincere before the Lord that I couldn't take being around him when I was living so terribly. One night he and Mom prayed a long time for me and waited up until I got home from my carousing.

"'Son, you're coming back to the Lord!' they said. 'God assured us in prayer tonight that it's just a matter of time. Hallelujah!' And they were right, as usual.

"My dad really walked with God. He was quite famous in his circle of churches, and everybody wanted him to speak. He was a good writer and became an elder statesman to a multitude of younger preachers and congregations. But all the acclaim and popularity, all the invitations and compliments, never affected him except to make him more humble before God. His heart was so humble before the Lord that he had a special power in prayer and in preaching. The Lord was really with my dad."

God can be with you and me in the same way as he was with Howard Goss, as we walk with humble hearts before him. Just as pride drives away the blessings of heaven and precedes certain failure, a humble heart is like a magnet that draws the favor of God towards us. The Lord really does dwell with certain

people in a special way. He is there because of the resting place provided for him by their humble hearts.

Let us humble our hearts before the Lord and seek his help and approval above all other things. Then by his grace we will personally experience the awesome power of his might as he surrounds us with blessings and favor.

FATHER, HELP US
TO HUMBLE OURSELVES
BEFORE YOU. SAVE US
FROM THE PRIDE AND
ARROGANCE THAT CUTS
US OFF FROM YOUR HAND
OF BLESSING. TEACH US
TO WALK SOFTLY EACH
DAY BEFORE YOU AND TO
NEVER LOSE SIGHT OF
YOUR GREATNESS AND
OUR NEED.

AMEN.

When any needy heart
begins to truly pray,
heaven itself stirs in response.

—SADHU SUNDAR SINGH

The LORD does not look at the
things man looks at. Man looks at
the outward appearance, but the
LORD looks at the heart.

—1 SAMUEL 16:7

Yield your hearts to the LORD.

—JOSHUA 24:23

Humble yourselves, therefore, under
God's mighty hand, that he may lift
you up in due time.

—1 PETER 5:6

REFINING OUR HEARTS

Many of us are quick to shout Hallelujah and celebrate God's blessings. Others of us have a sound intellectual grasp of Bible doctrine. That is all good—but we can easily avoid the fact that all the noise and knowledge in the world will take us nowhere if there is unremoved dross in our lives. All the talking in the world won't produce a godly life without the Lord's intimate, ongoing refining process in our hearts.

Some of us are overextended financially. Others of us have a calendar that is way too busy. The only way to get healthy is to reduce the indebtedness, to cut back the busyness. Whatever clutters our walk with God becomes the target of his purging process.

So many of us think that the more we do and the more we acquire, the happier we will be. Wrong! This is why so many Christians do not see God's purposes worked out in their lives. They can quote the Bible verse about the peace of God that passes all understanding, but they have little experience of what it means.

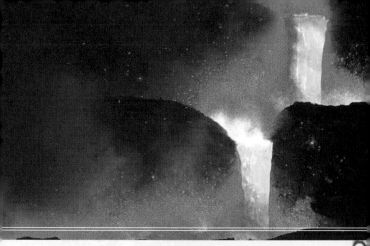

Because God loves you, he will always be direct with you. He tells you the truth. He is absolutely ruthless in going after the things that spoil the flow of his grace and blessing into our lives. His process is to subtract in order to add.

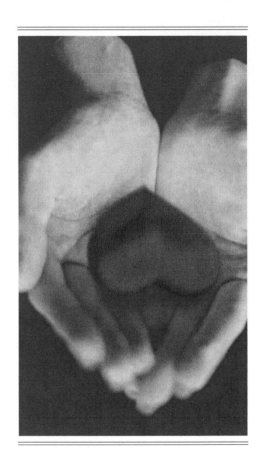

Lord, my heart is not large

enough,

my memory is not good enough,

my will is not strong enough:

Take my heart and enlarge it,

Take my memory and give it

quicker recall,

Take my will and make it strong

and make me conscious of Thee

ever present,

ever accompanying.

THE SENSITIVE HEART

Although a sensitive heart makes us
vulnerable in other aspects of life,
it is essential and leads to great blessing
when we're dealing with the Lord.
In fact, the cold, mechanical professionalism
that is admired in many fields of work will
actually lead us into trouble in the realm of
spiritual living. The Scriptures are filled with
warnings about a callous, insensitive, and hard
heart toward the Lord. We are never to stop
feeling things as we serve Christ. In fact,
our tenderness in response to things like
God's love, our own sin, and the needs
of others will become more acute as we grow
closer to the Lord. This is one of the signs
of a devoted godly life.

*Blessings can either humble us
and draw us closer to God,
or allow us to become full of pride
and self-sufficiency.*

O LORD Almighty,
blessed is the man who trusts in you.

—PSALM 84:12

As God's chosen people, holy and dearly
loved, clothe yourselves with compassion,
kindness, humility, gentleness and patience.

—COLOSSIANS 3:12

Return to the Lord your God,
for he is gracious and compassionate,
slow to anger and abounding in love.

—JOEL 2:13

The heart is also of critical importance
in a spiritual sense. The church, and
especially the pulpit that God blesses,
has to have a unique kind of heart.
I believe the heart factor is the most
overlooked aspect of all our sincere
searching for keys to living successfully
for Jesus Christ.

More is less
if God does not bless.

GOD'S WALL OF BLESSING

Uzziah's reign as the king of Judah began with great success and promise. A long, uninterrupted series of victories and national improvements spread his fame all the way to Egypt. But Uzziah was more than just a military leader. He oversaw the vast enterprises of livestock and farming that prospered during his reign. Fields and vineyards, hills and fertile lands were all affected by his progressive programs and love for the land. Uzziah was no narrow-minded man; he was a king noted for his diverse interests and unusual intelligence.

Do you know the secret behind Uzziah's ability to succeed in everything he endeavored to do? The Bible gives the exact, very simple reason for Uzziah's success: "God helped him" (2 Chronicles 26:7). Whatever challenges or battles King Uzziah faced, God surrounded him with a wall of blessing. No matter which angle anyone took to attack Judah, or which difficulties arose, the Lord was there to help this extraordinary king. To attack Uzziah meant you had to take on God first!

God's blessing was the secret behind all of

Uzziah's success. But was there a reason why God showed him such unusual favor? The Bible clearly affirms that the events leading to Uzziah's success were not accidents of providence. Rather, they were the result of something Uzziah was habitually doing. Scripture reveals that "he [Uzziah] continued to seek God in the days of Zechariah, who had understanding through the vision of God; and as long as he [Uzziah] sought the LORD, God prospered him" (2 Chronicles 26:5 nasb). As long as the king humbly looked to God for guidance and protection, he was pushed forward, surrounded, helped, and blessed by the Almighty. Who would not want to live as the object of that kind of a smile from heaven?

Under Zechariah's godly influence, Uzziah was doing two essential things. First he was seeking help from Almighty God. The king was conscious of his weakness and his inability to rule Judah rightly in his own strength. He knew that he needed God's direct assistance. This humble recognition of need is at the heart of all real prayer and provides the motivation for spending time in God's presence. Uzziah must have spent much time with the Lord because his tender heart knew no other source of help. How much we need to follow his example by praying every day, "Oh, Lord, I need your help. I can't make it without you."

As he sought God, Uzziah was seeking not only the Lord's help but also his approval. Desiring God's approval is the other half of the seeking that brought Uzziah such blessing. Seeking after God is a two-pronged endeavor. It requires not only the humility to say, "God, I need you," but also a heart that desires a pure life that is pleasing to the Lord. As long as King Uzziah sought God in both these ways, it was impossible for anyone or anything to bring him down.

Uzziah's humble heart was not bent on sinful self-seeking but rather on pleasing God, and this is what brought heaven's favor upon him.

The Scriptures continually encourage
us to open our hearts to God
in real prayer so that
he can answer us and provide
the blessings we desperately need.

I FIND THEE THRONED IN MY HEART,
my LORD JESUS.
IT IS ENOUGH.
I KNOW THAT THOU ART THRONED
IN HEAVEN.
MY HEART AND HEAVEN ARE ONE.

Trust in the LORD with all your heart
  and lean not on your own understanding;
In all your ways acknowledge him,
  and he will make your paths straight.

—PROVERBS 3:5-6

The ... Lord ... richly blesses all
who call on him.

—ROMANS 10:12

Search me, O God, and know my heart;
  test me and know my anxious thoughts.
See if there is any offensive way in me,
  and lead me in the way everlasting.

—PSALM 139:23-24

A CHILDLIKE HEART

God's eyes still roam over the earth looking for attentive, submissive hearts so he can show himself strong and mighty on our behalf. Let's ask God for the blessing of a childlike heart such as young Samuel had, so that when the Lord calls our name we, too, can answer, "Speak, LORD for your servant is listening" (1 Samuel 3:9).

Lord, help us to have a listening heart
that is soft and teachable. Save us from
being so filled with ourselves that we
can't hear you. Give us the grace to both
listen and obey when you speak to us.
Amen.

MAY THE LORD BLESS YOU WITH ALL
GOOD AND KEEP YOU FROM ALL EVIL;
MAY HE GIVE LIGHT TO YOUR HEART
WITH LOVING WISDOM, AND BE GRACIOUS
TO YOU WITH ETERNAL KNOWLEDGE;
MAY HE LIFT UP HIS LOVING COUNTE-
NANCE UPON YOU FOR ETERNAL PEACE.

Every good
and perfect gift
is from above,
coming down from
the Father of
the heavenly lights.
—James 1:17

THE SOURCE
OF ALL
BLESSINGS

HEARTS IN SYNC

A heart out of tune, out of sync
with God's heart, will produce a life
of spiritual barrenness and missed
opportunities. But as we ask the Lord
to bring our hearts into harmony
with and submission to his, we will
find the secret of his blessings that
has remained the same throughout
all generations.

The Holy Spirit has been sent to lift up our
heads, no matter the circumstances, and fulfill
the word spoken by the prophet so long ago:

*"Gladness and joy will overtake them,
and sorrow and sighing will flee away."*

ISAIAH 51:11

A SIMPLE EQUATION

God has given us a very simple equation if only we have the faith to reach out and experience it:

1. The Holy Spirit's power is our greatest need.
2. This power and blessing is freely promised to all of God's people.
3. This promise can only be fully received through sincere praying in faith and through waiting on God for his blessing to come.

This is what happened in the New Testament, and this is the only thing that will satisfy our soul's thirst.

You also were included in Christ when you heard the word of truth, the gospel of your salvation. Having believed, you were marked in him with a seal, the promised Holy Spirit, who is a deposit guaranteeing our inheritance until the redemption of those who are God's possession—to the praise of his glory.

—EPHESIANS 1:13–14

Build yourselves up in your most holy faith and pray in the Holy Spirit. Keep yourselves in God's love as you wait for the mercy of our Lord Jesus Christ to bring you to eternal life.

—JUDE 20–21

If any of you lacks wisdom, he should ask God, who gives generously to all without finding fault, and it will be given to him.

—JAMES 1:5

A MIGHTY WOMAN
OF GOD

Among the mighty warriors of faith I have
had the privilege of knowing during my years of
ministry, I count Delores Bonner. Delores is an
African-American woman who lives alone in
Bedford-Stuyvesant, one of Brooklyn's toughest
neighborhoods. She has been a medical technician
at Maimonides Hospital for more than thirty years.
Carol and I met her one year at Christmastime
while we were bringing gifts to some poor children
in our congregation.

Delores had a full apartment that day—but
these children were not hers. She had brought
them from a nearby shelter to meet us. Their
natural mother was too consumed with her own
problems to be present even for an occasion such
as this.

"How did you come to meet these children?"
I asked.

Delores modestly mumbled something that
didn't really answer my questions. Only from
others did I learn that right after her conversion
in a prayer meeting at the church in 1982, she
became concerned for children in the streets and
in the crack houses. God touched her heart, and
she started bringing the children to Sunday school.

At first she packed them into taxis; later on someone heard what she was doing and bought her a car. Today she has a van so she can transport more children and teenagers to hear the gospel.

This is only part of Delores's story. On Sunday's between services, she oversees the crew that cleans the sanctuary so it will be ready for the next crowd. On Saturdays she goes out with the evangelism teams, knocking on doors in the housing projects to share God's love.

On weekdays I find her on her knees upstairs with the Prayer Band, taking a shift to intercede for people's needs. She did the same thing on a ministry trip to Peru, where she joined others in calling out to God on my behalf as I preached in an outdoor meeting.

When we honored Delores as the Brooklyn Tabernacle's "Woman of the Year," she was embarrassed and said little. But the whole church knows that living among us is a mighty woman of

God whose fame transcends the world's
shallow value system.

Delores is a woman of quiet
determination, the kind in whom the merging
of divine and human effort is clearly shown.
Wayward children and broken marriages will
be touched by the hand of God only as
someone like Delores stands in the gap and
fights valiantly in the power of the Spirit.

The acid test
of spiritual growth
is love,
and love always means
living for others.

Almighty God, Father of our
   Lord Jesus Christ,
   grant, we pray, that we
   might be grounded
   and settled in your
   truth by the coming of
   your Holy Spirit into
   our hearts.
What we do not know,
   reveal to us;
What is lacking within us,
   make complete;
That which we do know,
   confirm in us;
And keep us blameless in
   your service,
   through Jesus Christ
   our Lord.

We rejoice in the hope of the glory of God. ... And hope does not disappoint us, because God has poured out his love into our hearts by the Holy Spirit, whom he has given us.

—ROMANS 5:2,5

THE HEAVENLY HELPER

The Holy Spirit is our helper because that's what he does and is supposed to do. The name helper shows us how we should think of the Holy Spirit. A helper fills a troubled heart with joy towards God. A helper encourages us to be happy that our sins have been forgiven, death has been conquered, heaven has been opened, and God is smiling upon us.

Whoever understands what it means for the Spirit to be our helper will have already won the battle. That person will find nothing but pure comfort and joy in heaven and on earth.

The Holy Spirit is the helper, and we are the troubled and timid ones whom he helps.

—MARTIN LUTHER
BY FAITH ALONE, AUG.16

Imitating God,
like listening to him,
is another quality
that aligns us
with his purposes
and makes room
for even more
of his blessings.

Living Abundantly Through God's Blessings

Thanks be to God! He gives us the victory
through our Lord Jesus Christ.

—1 CORINTHIANS 15:57

Jesus said, "When he, the Spirit of truth, comes,
he will guide you into all truth. He will not
speak on his own; he will speak only what he
hears, and he will tell you what is yet to come."

—JOHN 16:13

The one whom God has sent speaks the words
of God, for God gives the Spirit without limit.

—JOHN 3:34

The LORD gives strength to his people;
the LORD blesses his people with peace.

—PSALM 29:11

Whenever God's Spirit
is working and blessing,
there will always be the sweet
fragrance of kindness.

DIVINE HELP,
DIVINE POWER

It is staggering to remember that Peter walked with Jesus for three years and received teaching, discipleship, and a moral example unparalleled in all of history. And yet all of that never made Peter the man God intended him to be. It is not until we see Peter "filled with the Holy Spirit" that things really turned around. No wonder Jesus excitedly assured them that greater days were coming for all of them when the Holy Spirit, their invisible Helper, came upon them in power.

Ministry is especially hopeless without the Holy Spirit. Our attempt at ministry will be an absolute exercise in futility if we are not expecting and experiencing divine help through the power of the Holy Spirit.

LED BY THE
HOLY SPIRIT

Twenty-five years ago while on a trip to
South America, I was invited to preach at one
of the largest churches in the capital of
Suriname and I looked forward to seeing my
Surinamese friend who pastored the
congregation.

Even though it was February,
temperatures were soaring as I was driven
to the church for the morning service. A few
ceiling fans turned slowly but did little to
combat the stifling heat and humidity. After
some preliminaries I was introduced to speak,
and within ten minutes my shirt and suit were
hanging on me soaked with perspiration. But
the heat was the least of my problems that
Sunday morning.

My sermon was bouncing back to me as
if I were preaching to a concrete wall! The
people were not inattentive, but a spiritual
hardness permeated the atmosphere. I struggled
mightily to get my message across. There was
something in the air much more oppressive
than the temperature and humidity. What was
wrong? I didn't know, but it made me try
harder, which only created more perspiration.

I started desperately praying in my heart even as I continued my sermon. God, I prayed silently, what am I up against here, and what can I do to bring a blessing to your people?

My message soon ended, and I asked the people to bow their heads in prayer. As we quietly waited before the Lord, my own heart was still asking God for direction. I opened my eyes to look out over the audience, and suddenly my attention was drawn to a blonde, middle-aged woman sitting in the last row. I can't define what I felt, other than that I sensed the Lord focusing on her. Knowing I should follow this vague leading from the Holy Spirit, I called her out publicly and asked if she would come forward for prayer.

The woman complied with my request, but as soon as she reached the altar area she broke down and began to weep. Soon many others walked forward to join her, and a prayer

meeting broke out. Everyone's heart was melted. The atmosphere was transformed into something quite beautiful and heavenly. As the organ quietly played a hymn, the Spirit of God "broke out" and created a 180-degree turn in the service.

I went to my pastor-friend's home afterward for dinner, and our hearts were rejoicing because of what God had done during the service. I didn't quite understand all that had taken place at the service until my friend explained:

"Brother Jim, our church has been suffering for months from a terrible outbreak of gossip and slander. Much of the nasty talk has been directed against my wife and me.

The woman you called forward was the ringleader and major source of this destructive

talk. When you called her out, it was as if God, through a total stranger, had singled her out in a supernatural way. Some others involved with her sensed that, they were also convicted. She hugged us at the end and begged for forgiveness. She confessed her sin and wants God to bring blessing to both herself and our church. Praise the Lord!"

A young, inexperienced preacher faced difficulty he didn't know how to handle, but God turned the whole situation around. How marvelous it is to serve the God who shows himself strong during our weakest moments!

Now to each one the manifestation of the Spirit is given for the common good. To one there is given through the Spirit the message of wisdom, to another the message of knowledge by means of the same Spirit, to another faith by the same Spirit, to another gifts of healing by that one Spirit, to another miraculous powers, to another prophecy, to another distinguishing between spirits, to another speaking in different kinds of tongues, and to still another the interpretation of tongues. All these are the work of one and the same Spirit, and he gives them to each one, just as he determines.

—1 CORINTHIANS 12:7–11

O God who dost teach the hearts

of thy faithful people by sending

to us the light of thy Holy

Spirit: Grant us by that same

Spirit to be enlightened in our

minds, sanctified in our hearts,

kindled in love and strengthened

by grace, through Jesus Christ,

thy blessed Son, our Lord.

THE TEMPLE OF
THE HOLY SPIRIT

We shouldn't doubt that the Holy Spirit lives in us, but we should certainly recognize that we are a temple of the Holy Spirit. If someone feels a love for God's Word and gladly hears, speaks, thinks, teaches, and writes about Christ, you should know that this doesn't come from a person's will or reason but from the Holy Spirit. It's impossible for this to happen without the Holy Spirit.

Those who have any kind of love and desire for the Word should gratefully acknowledge that these attitudes are poured into them by the Holy Spirit. For we are not born with these attitudes and cannot acquire them through the law. This transformation rests completely and absolutely in the hand of the Almighty.

—MARTIN LUTHER
BY FAITH ALONE, OCT 13

GOD'S MESSAGE
OF LOVE

God intended his work—everything from
teaching a Sunday school class to pioneering a
brand-new missionary effort—to be marked
by a similar flow of a spiritual kind. The Bible
calls it being "led by the Spirit" (Romans 8:14;
Galatians 5:18). Yes, there are important
doctrinal principles to learn and biblical facts
to nail down, but at the same time, only God
the Holy Spirit can weave them all together in
a seamless, almost unconscious way so we can
touch people with God's message of love.

What we need is that unique merger
of divine truth, human personality, and
Holy Spirit gifting that produces effective
ministry for Christ.

Jesus said, "I will ask the Father, and he will give you another Counselor to be with you forever—the Spirit of truth."

—JOHN 14:16

Do you not know that your body is a temple of the Holy Spirit, who is in you, whom you have received from God? You are not your own; you were bought at a price.

—1 CORINTHIANS 6:19–20

God sent the Spirit of his Son into our hearts, the Spirit who calls out, "Abba, Father."

—GALATIANS 4:6

YIELD TO THE SPIRIT

The Apostle Paul's plans to evangelize in certain areas were subject to the Holy Spirit's intervention. "Paul and his companions traveled throughout the region of Phrygia and Galatia, having been kept by the Holy Spirit from preaching the word in the province of Asia" (Acts 16:6). This is one of the beautiful secrets of the church and ministry God blesses. The people know that God's desire to lead his people by the Spirit has not changed, so they seek to remain sensitive to his voice. How else can God's people accomplish God's will except by being led by God's Spirit? Who wants to mechanically follow dead church traditions or man-made formulas when we can have God take us by his hand and guide us?

Being led by the Spirit was not an unusual experience for Paul, as we see in the next verse: "When they came to the border of Mysia, they tried to enter Bithynia, but the Spirit of Jesus would not allow them to" (v.7). Paul was not planning a vacation in Bithynia. He was planning to preach the gospel in a province that needed to hear it. Even so, the Spirit of Jesus had other plans for the apostle, and he obeyed in childlike fashion.

Oh, how we need to follow the example of Paul's tender submission to the promptings of the Holy Spirit! Others may call such devotion fanaticism or emotionalism, but the people God blesses believe their Bibles. They know that the Holy Spirit has not changed one iota in two thousand years. What he did then for Paul he will do for us as we yield our hearts to him and learn to listen.

O HOLY SPIRIT, WHOSE
PRESENCE IS LIBERTY,
GRANT US THAT FREEDOM OF
THE SPIRIT,
WHICH WILL NOT FEAR TO
TREAD IN UNKNOWN WAYS,
NOR BE HELD BACK BY MIS-
GIVINGS OF OURSELVES AND
FEAR OF OTHERS.
EVER BECKON US FORWARD TO
THE PLACE OF THY WILL
WHICH IS ALSO THE PLACE
OF THY POWER,
O EVER-LEADING, EVER-
LOVING LORD.

THE SPIRIT SPEAKS
WITH PURPOSE

Two summers ago in a Sunday afternoon service, I took a seat on the front pew in order to better enjoy the choir's ministry as they sang their opening songs. The first song was about God's great redeeming love. I closed my eyes and let the words sink in.

Somewhere along about the second verse, I sensed the Holy Spirit saying to me, Go and preach the gospel—right now. Go up and tell them of God's love.

At first I thought I was maybe just getting a little emotional about an inspirational song. Or maybe Satan was tempting me into some kind of weird behavior.

Then I thought, My goodness, we haven't even taken the offering yet! This isn't the time to preach and given an invitation; that comes at the end of a meeting, not this early. But the impression would not go away. In another thirty seconds I felt that if I did not respond, I would be grieving the Holy Spirit. I silently prayed, God, I don't want to fail you by not doing your will. I'm going up there at the end of this song. Somehow stop me if I'm wrong. I felt I had to obey, but I was still nervous about interrupting the meeting.

As the final chord was resolving, I quickly moved up the steps and onto the platform. My wife Carol glanced at me with a quizzical look on her face. I took the microphone and asked Calvin Hunt to tell the people briefly what God had done in his life. He went into his story of terrible addiction to crack cocaine and how God had set him free. When he finished, I spoke for about ten minutes about the gospel

and proceeded to give an invitation. The organist played softly; the choir stayed quietly in place through all this, just waiting to see what would happen next. From all over the auditorium, dozens of people began coming forward to the altar. The sound of weeping could be heard as people were moved upon by the Spirit and now turned to Christ. We prayed with them all, and it was a blessed time of spiritual harvest. Conviction seemed deep and real as the Holy Spirit blessed the simple gospel message.

Eventually I told them to return to their seats, saying, "Well, we haven't taken the offering yet. Let's do that as the choir sings another song." The meeting continued on to its conclusion.

Sometime that following week, the phone rang in our church offices and a gentleman from Texas shared his story with us:

"My family and I were just on a visit to New York for the weekend. We have a nineteen-year-old son who has totally hardened to the things of the Lord and we wanted to bring him on Sunday to your church in hopes that God would somehow reach him. On Sunday I checked our airline tickets once again and realized I'd made a terrible mistake. We wouldn't be able to stay for the whole service—or else we'd miss our flight home.

"I was kicking myself for not planning better, but then early in the service out of nowhere—your pastor walked up onto the platform and started to share the gospel.

Suddenly my son was standing up with the others and heading for the altar! He just broke down before the Lord, calling out to God for forgiveness. When he came back to the seat, he was a different person. My wife and I are overjoyed for the great thing God has done."

God knows things we have no way of knowing. When we don't inquire of the Lord and ask in faith for guidance, we totally miss what he wants to accomplish.

Jesus said, "You will receive power
when the Holy Spirit comes on you;
and you will be my witnesses in
Jerusalem, and in all Judea and Samaria,
and to the ends of the earth."

—ACTS 1:8

THE UNIQUENESS
OF CHRISTIANITY

This is unique among the world's
religions: that men and women have
become the human temples of God's
very presence. They have been filled up
with the Holy Spirit the way Solomon's
temple was once filled up with smoke.
Buddhism, Islam, and the rest pay
honor and respect to a god, or gods.
But the gods remain "out there" at a
safe distance; they don't come and
fill up redeemed worshipers
in an intimate, dynamic way.
This is the unique note of Christianity.

The Lord is eager to make spiritual changes
among us and shower us with his blessings.
He wants us—his people—to experience the
greatness of his power and the depth of his
love in a new way. All he needs from us is a
listening ear and a heart that believes that
with God all things are possible.

WAITING
FOR GOD'S
BLESSING

We wait for the blessed hope —
the glorious appearing of
our great God and Savior,
Jesus Christ. —Titus 2:13

The people blessed by God
must persevere no matter what.
They must understand that
Satan fights the hardest
when the greatest spiritual
breakthroughs and blessings
are just around the corner.
God has begun a good work in us,
and he will bring it to completion
as we wait in faith.

GOD'S TIME OF FAVOR

A few years ago, the Brooklyn Tabernacle
faced a new challenge that forced us to trust
God in a greater dimension than ever before.
Motivated by God's promptings and four
overcrowded services every Sunday, the
leadership of our congregation purchased a
four-thousand-seat theater, along with two
connected buildings, even though we had no
money when negotiations began. God provided
in incredible ways, but the scope of renovation
was tremendous, needing a budget of millions
of dollars!

Although the situation did not look
favorable, the Lord continued to help us.
Large, unsolicited gifts came in along with the

regular giving of both the congregation and friends around the country. As the demolition stage was ending, I went to South America with Carol and a small missions team. Just before I left for that trip, I had received a call from the organization that was lending us money. Even with their loan, the official informed me, there was a six-million-dollar shortfall! While I was in South America, that six-million-dollar figure started to get my attention. Where will we get that kind of money? What am I doing to raise this money?

I know of only two ways to raise large sums of money: pray and give. One afternoon I took a walk to pray. Instead of focusing on

God, however, I began thinking of all the
appeal letters I should probably be writing.
As I churned inside, I sensed God speaking
to my heart. "Leave it with me," he seemed to
say. "Don't worry. Just trust, pray, and wait."
Every time I was tempted to be anxious,
I would sense the same message: "Wait on me.
Don't try to solve it yourself. Just wait."
I began again to rest in the Lord.

Only hours after returning to New York
City I went to the church.
My desk was piled high with
mail, faxes, and phone messages.
I started working.
By late afternoon
I opened two letters
within the space of ten
minutes that made my
heart leap for joy. One was
from a man in the Midwest
who said that God had
impressed him to give us one
million dollars for the new
campus project. The second letter
was from a group I had never met
who informed me they would give
us five million dollars!

Both gifts were unsolicited. The
gifts totaled exactly six million dollars—

the very amount with which I had struggled!
The Lord obviously had not forgotten us while
we were busy doing his work in South America.
Nor had he forgotten the rest of the congregation
praying at home. God's "time of favor" had
come; he helped us just as he had promised.
We also learned another valuable lesson: when
God's people believe and pray, the Lord will
provide, but we must learn to wait on him with
faithful, obedient hearts until the answer comes.

Which lesson of faith is God seeking to
teach you? Are you willing to trust him with
the problems and heartaches you are facing
today? He is waiting for you to transfer
your problems . . . doubts . . . pain . . . and
challenges into his hand in total trust.

Don't forget—he works for those who wait!

HEAVENLY FATHER, WE PRAISE
YOU FOR ALL THE GRACE AND
MERCY YOU HAVE SHOWN US IN
THE PAST. TEACH US TO PRAY
MORE AND TRUST IN YOU WITH ALL
OUR HEARTS. GIVE US THE KIND
OF FAITH THAT WILL WAIT
PATIENTLY FOR THE FULFILLMENT
OF YOUR PROMISES. HELP US TO
HUMBLE OURSELVES BEFORE YOU
AND LISTEN CAREFULLY TO YOUR
WORD. MAKE US A HOLY AND
COMPASSIONATE PEOPLE SO THAT
OTHERS CAN SEE JESUS IN OUR
LIVES. WE WANT OUR HEARTS TO
BE YOUR SPECIAL HOME. IN
CHRIST'S NAME.
AMEN.

The LORD longs to be gracious to you;
he rises to show you compassion.
For the LORD is a God of justice.
Blessed are all who wait for him!

—ISAIAH 30:18

Hope that is seen is no hope at all. Who
hopes for what he already has? But if we
hope for what we do not yet have, we wait
for it patiently.

—ROMANS 8:24–25

By faith we eagerly await through the
Spirit the righteousness for which we hope.

—GALATIANS 5:5

*The battle of the
Christian life has always been
not just to believe,
but to keep on believing.
This is how we will
grow strong in faith
and see the actual fulfillment
of God's promises in our lives.*

PATIENTLY ENDURE

God will take care of us

in good and bad times.

We shouldn't become

over confident in

times of plenty, but we also

need to patiently endure

times of adversity.

God will never leave us.

He will be near us

in our troubles.

Unbelievers don't have

this confidence in God

because they put their trust

in earthly things.

—MARTIN LUTHER

BY FAITH ALONE, AUG. 17

SEEKING GOD'S
BLESSING

Although he was God's anointed king and
a veteran warrior, although the Lord had
helped him countless times before, David
would not move without God's approval and
promise of blessing. No wonder David had
such a special place in the heart of Jehovah!

Those of us who want to see God fighting
our battles must pause and contemplate all of
this very carefully. There is no "automatic
pilot" by which we can run our lives. We
constantly need the Lord's direction as we face
all the decisions of life. We can't live off past
successes either, because there is no guarantee
that we will have God's approval and blessing
on our next venture. Neither can we run
around reciting "God is with me, God is with
me," because the Lord was never with any
king more than David, yet David still had to
see God for fresh instructions.

Somehow, in some way, the Lord will
guide our steps in the way we should go.
He will honor our desire to seek his will
and blessing.

The Lord will
guide you always.

—ISAIAH 58:11

As for me, I watch in hope for the LORD,
I wait for God my Savior;
my God will hear me.

—MICAH 7:7

The blessing of the Lord brings wealth,
and he adds no trouble to it.

—PROVERBS 10:22

I wait for the Lord, my soul waits,
and in his word I put my hope.

—PSALM 130:5

GOD IS UP TO
SOMETHING GREAT

If God is for us, who can be against us? God's plan to use us for his glory cannot be thwarted by any weapon formed against us. Opposition, jealousy, and hatred should never cause us to become discouraged. Rather, these things ought to cause us to rejoice that God is up to something great! Why else would Satan go to such lengths to discourage us and tempt us to look away from God's sure promises?

Don't quit believing today in what God has made real to your heart. No matter how unlikely or even hopeless the situation seems to be, God is able to fulfill his word concerning your life, your ministry, and your church.

MAY THE LOVE OF THE LORD JESUS

DRAW US TO HIMSELF;

MAY THE POWER OF THE

LORD JESUS

STRENGTHEN US IN HIS SERVICE;

MAY THE JOY OF THE LORD JESUS

FILL OUR SOULS.

MAY THE BLESSING OF GOD ALMIGHTY,

THE FATHER, THE SON, AND THE

HOLY GHOST,

BE AMONGST YOU

AND REMAIN WITH YOU

ALWAYS.

THE MYSTERY OF GOD'S TIMING

Wendy Alvear grew up in Brooklyn and characterized herself as "a romantic," dreaming of the day she would get married to a handsome husband and raise a houseful of children of her own. Her sunny disposition was only partly suppressed by the strict-minded Spanish church she attended three or four nights a week. By the time she was an adolescent she stopped going to church.

By her senior year, Wendy's life was taken up with dance clubs, smoking, and drinking — but "no hard drugs," she affirmed to God. Her first real boyfriend was battling to overcome heroin. "I would plead with him not to do drugs.

So as a compromise, we'd drink wine together instead." Wendy thus became a steady drinker.

Her next boyfriend was better. John was drug-free and had a job as a shoe salesman. "Here was the man of my dreams," Wendy says. "When we got engaged on Valentine's Day, it was the highlight of my life." But within three months Wendy learned that John was seeking sexual favors elsewhere. She promptly broke the engagement.

"Now I was really lonely," she says. "And I wasn't close enough to God to ask for his help. I sank into more drinking, which made me angry and aggressive. I gradually withdrew into depression and stayed in my room."

This unhappy lifestyle continued until Wendy was twenty-five, and finally ready to listen to the Lord. A great relief swept over her spirit. She started to grow in the Lord, build Christian friendships, join the singles group, and sing in the choir at the Brooklyn Tabernacle. Years went by. Inside, Wendy's desire to be married was as strong as ever.

Yet God seemed not to give an answer to her heartfelt question, Okay, God—where is he?

One day, after her thirty-fifth birthday, Wendy set aside time to seek the Lord. "All right, Lord— I will place my desire for a husband 'on the altar,' I will give it to you. Go ahead and burn it up like a sacrifice. Consume it! I will stop whining about this." Peace came back into her soul and Wendy went on with her life.

About a year later, a man came to one of our daughter churches for an appointment. His name was John Alvear—the same John who had been in Wendy's life years before. Soon John showed up at the Brooklyn Tabernacle, looking for Wendy. She avoided John for a good while. She discovered that John's attitude had indeed changed; he had become a new creation in Christ. He and

Wendy began dating, and a warm affection blossomed.

But Wendy was still concerned about getting involved and sought my advice. I told her, "Don't be afraid of what God is doing in your life. John is a very special man."

And that is how, at the age of thirty-seven, Wendy finally became a bride. Their wedding was an explosion of joy. They now have two children and a home in the borough of Staten Island.

Wendy advises others, "Whatever you do, keep seeking God's will for your life. He will do it! Don't settle for anything less. Wait for God—he knows how to give you the best."

I am blessed
over and over again
when I see God
unfolding his plans
as his people wait
in faith with open hearts
to receive from him.

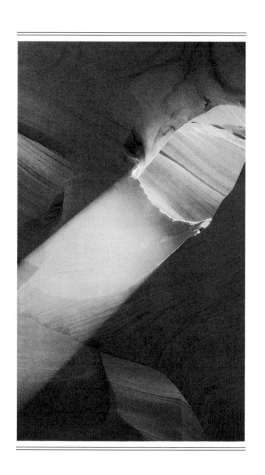

Be still before the Lord and wait
*   patiently for him;*
do not fret when men succeed in
*   their ways,*
when they carry out their wicked
*   schemes.*
Refrain from anger and turn from wrath;
*   do not fret—it leads only to evil.*
For evil men will be cut off,
*   but those who hope in the Lord*
*   will inherit the land.*

—PSALM 37:7–9

Let me depend on God alone:

who never changes,

who knows what is best for me

so much better than I;

And gives in a thousand ways,

at all times

all that the perfect Father can

for the son's good growth,

things needful, things salutary,

things wise, beneficent and happy.

RELY ON GOD'S PROMISES

If what we need isn't available to us, we have to

rely on God's promises. If we don't rely on God,

we are testing him. When we try to dictate to God

the time, place, and manner for him to act,

we are testing him. At the same time, we're trying

to see if he is really there. Doing that is putting

limits on God and trying to make him do what

we want. It's nothing less than trying to deprive

God of his divinity. But we must realize that

God is free — not subject to any limitations.

He must dictate to us the place, manner, and time.

—MARTIN LUTHER
BY FAITH ALONE, AUG.17

The secret is to have a heart
that waits on the Lord,
to keep waiting in faith
and glad expectation for
the things he has promised.

KEEP ON WAITING

The challenge before us is to have faith in God, and the hardest part of faith is the waiting. Jesus laid down as a first principle, "According to your faith will it be done to you" (Matthew 9:29). But to receive the blessing we need, we must believe and keep on believing, to wait and keep on waiting. We need to wait in prayer, wait with our Bibles open as we confess his promises, wait in joyful praise and worship of the God who will never forget our case, and wait as we continue serving others in his name.

Wait for the Lord;
    be strong and take heart
    and wait for the Lord.

    —PSALM 27:14

The Sovereign LORD says, ...
"I will bless them and the places
    surrounding my hill. I will
    send down showers in season;
there will be showers of blessing."

    —EZEKIEL 34:20, 26

The Lord is good to those whose
        hope is in him,
    to the one who seeks him;
it is good to wait quietly
        for the salvation of the Lord.

    —LAMENTATIONS 3:25–26

When we honestly
confess our sins,
we clear the way
for fresh blessings
to come upon us
from the Lord.

If anyone is in Christ,
he is a new creation;
the old has gone,
the new has come!
—2 Corinthians 5:17

GOD'S BLESSINGS CHANGE LIVES

SEEK GOD CONTINUALLY

We must stay in close communion with our Lord if we are to enjoy his full blessing. Reflex responses based on past success are not adequate, because we need to continually seek God for fresh guidance. We also need to be sensitive to the Lord's timing concerning our actions. Often we pursue God's will about something but don't have the faith to see his timing for it as well. As we wait before the Lord, we will learn to "hear the sound" of the Holy Spirit's voice in our hearts and move out into God's perfect plan for us.

GOD USES
"DAMAGED GOODS"

Denise Tsikudo is a short little woman in our church who came to the Lord in early 1993. At that time she was a single mother with two daughters; she had no particular religious background other than a stint in witchcraft. Her recreational drug use had increased, and so had her binge drinking, to two or three times a week, which created a sense of depression. It was this dilemma that nudged her toward coming to church, where she soon gave her heart to Christ.

She stopped all drinking. She quit chain-smoking. But did everything run smoothly thereafter?

Within just a few months, while she was still a baby believer, Denise suffered the sudden loss of her mother. There was no warning. Denise found her dead on the bathroom floor. Denise had to sort out her mother's legal affairs, a complicated task.

Disagreements arose among the relatives. Her sisters and brothers rebuffed her. Her friends were critical of how much time she was spending in church. At the end of July that year, after returning home from a Bible class she settled into bed for a comfortable sleep. The next morning when Denise opened her eyes there in the doorway stood a stranger with his T-shirt pulled up over the bridge of his nose. Only his two fearsome eyes could be seen. In his right hand was a silver revolver.

Denise prayed as the man pushed a pillow over her face. In the ugly moments that followed, Denise saw the gun lying on the bed no more than inches from her head. When her attacker finally left, Denise sat up, quivering. She called 911. Over the next few weeks Denise decided to move to her mother's vacant house in Bedford-Stuyvesant. That next winter the roofed leaked, the boiler broke and one of the girls contracted chicken pox. What else could possibly go wrong?

It was soon after her assault, while Denise was still somewhat traumatized and afraid to go out much, that she managed to make it to one of our Sunday services. Choir auditions were announced that day and Denise somehow got the courage to fill out an application. After passing the vocal test, Denise interviewed with Carol to whom she opened up and shared the

horrific, still painful events of the recent past: the rape, the terror, the fear and trauma.

Later Carol shared Denise's story with me and together we agree that even though Denise was "damaged goods" the Lord wanted to use her in the choir.

As the choir sang the next Sunday, I searched for Denise. There she was, properly looking at Carol, singing all the words—with no expression whatsoever. But over time, the Lord began using the other members of the choir to lift Denise up from her pain. The challenges of the winter and the other difficulties did not disappear overnight. But she began to evidence a new spirit about her.

Months later, I began looking again for Denise. There she was in the front row with a joyful radiance on her face, hands lifted high.

The lady who could not even smile or look at me was gone forever. I wept openly at God's ability to bring her through all kinds of difficulties with victory and joy on the other side.

God does not always take us out of difficulty; many times he takes us through it. The first shows us God's power, which is omnipotent. The second teaches us the patience, character, and tenderness we need to bless others.

You were taught, with regard to your former
way of life, to put off your old self, which
is being corrupted by its deceitful desires;
to be made new in the attitude of your minds;
and to put on the new self, created to be like
God in true righteousness and holiness.

—EPHESIANS 4:22–24

The Spirit of the LORD will come upon
you in power, ... and you will be changed
into a different person.

—1 SAMUEL 10:6

SIMPLE ESSENTIALS

The blessing of God always depends
on the simple essentials of spiritual life.
You don't need a seminary education
or an especially gifted mind to learn the
secret of his favor. In fact, a humble
Christian in the most impoverished
or limited circumstances can experience
more divine blessing than a brilliant
theologian surrounded by a vast library
of religious books. It's the simple devotion
of the heart, not complicated concepts,
that opens up the windows of heaven's
blessing upon our souls.

Father, we bring all our failures to you in Jesus' name. We have tried so hard and so often to change. But our problems are too big for us to handle. Today, we give up and throw ourselves totally on your love and mercy. Cleanse us and change us from the inside out. Teach us how to imitate you—to have your heart of kindness and mercy. Teach us to walk in the Spirit every day so we can know your power and victory. We rest in your mercy and faithfulness. Amen.

Confession of sin
is the most important key
to being a people and church
that lives continually
under the blessing of heaven.

UNDESERVED
BLESSINGS

People in the world today receive good things

because Christians are living faithfully

on the earth. So we should be encouraged

and comforted when we see God's blessings.

It proves that the church is still present

on earth and that God's people,

though small in number, haven't disappeared

completely. It's for the sake of Christians

that God shows his undeserved kindness

to everyone in the world.

—MARTIN LUTHER
BY FAITH ALONE, NOV. 25

CHANGING A LIFESTYLE

Born and raised in the "hood" of southeast Washington, D.C., Steve nevertheless excelled in school and earned a scholarship to a Pennsylvania prep academy. While living there in his mid-teen years, he confessed to a counselor that he felt a vague attraction to other boys and didn't know what to think about that. The counselor answered that this was all very natural and was nothing to worry about. Steve wasn't convinced, but he said nothing more.

Steve's good grades next brought him a scholarship to Dartmouth University. His first actual homosexual experience came as a freshman.

"The next morning, I felt so hollow, so empty," Steve remembers. " I had been reaching out for love, but it didn't satisfy." Later, thinking to himself that he had certainly gotten off tract, a voice suddenly said to him, Get out of it! Steve did not heed the warning, and without any other spiritual anchor in his life, he yielded to his homosexual impulses again and again.

Steve's talent in dance earned him yet another scholarship, this one at the world-renowned Alvin Ailey American Dance Center in New York City. He shared an apartment with four other dance students—all of them gay. A close camaraderie developed in the group. Meanwhile, a cousin challenged Steve to at least read the Bible and it took him a year and a half to reach Revelation.

Steve went from one liaison to another, until a relationship solidified with a very talented artist. The two picked out an apartment to share together—one block from the Brooklyn Tabernacle. In October, 1980, Steve finally visited the church.

"I felt the love of God the minute I came through the door," he says. Steve kept coming back.

About that time, a big Gay Pride parade was scheduled in the city, and Steve's friends urged him to go. "I watched the crowds of gays, and I never felt so alone in all my life. God was steadily chiseling away at my beliefs."

The struggle with his emotions continued; there was no quick exit from the gay lifestyle for Steve. He grew depressed at times and lost a lot of weight. But he was determined to

believe that God would change him on the
inside. He made the tough decision to stop all
gay activity. Then one day, for no apparent
reason, he felt a release from his bondage. "
All of a sudden, I just knew that Jesus had
set me free!" he says.

The relationship with his partner dissolved.
Steve joined a prayer group where he found
spiritual encouragement, and his life began to
overflow with the Holy Spirit.

In a few years, Steve met a young Christian
woman named Desiree in our church. In time
they fell in love and were married. Desiree
knew everything there was to know about
Steve—and never flinched. Together they
started a support group for people with HIV
and AIDS. Many were led to the Lord and

taught that living for Christ is walking in faith and joy according to God's plan.

Steve and Desiree now have a home near a well-known East Coast college where Steve is an assistant professor. Two darling little girls have been born to grace their home as more evidence of God's wonderful love. God's hand is on this couple and their children in a special way.

There is not a doubt in my mind that this wonderful man has been changed by the power of God.

Enter my heart, O Holy Spirit,
   come in blessed mercy and
   set me free.
Throw open, O Lord, the locked
doors of my mind;
   cleanse the chambers of my
   thought for thy dwelling:
   light there the fires of thine
   own holy brightness
      in new understandings
      of truth.
O Holy Spirit, very God, whose
presence is liberty,
   grant me the perfect freedom
      to be thy servant
      today, tomorrow, evermore.

This is what the Sovereign LORD says, ...
"I will give you a new heart and put a
new spirit in you; I will remove
from you your heart of stone
and give you a heart of flesh.
And I will put my Spirit in you
and move you to follow my decrees
and be careful to keep my laws."

—EZEKIEL 36:22,26–27

In my anguish I cried to the LORD,
and he answered by setting me free.

—PSALM 118:5

BREAKOUT POWER

When we consult the Lord concerning his will for our lives and when we desire his presence above all else, the result will be "breakout" power. What an experience it is to have God working on behalf of his people while they fight on bravely in his name!

Possibly you face a dilemma of some kind today. Maybe it is related to your marriage or a son or daughter who is not serving God. Or possibly you need the Lord to heal you in the realm of your emotions. Whatever the case, remember that we have a God who can "break out" and supernaturally help us. And it all begins when we slow down and humble ourselves in prayer. We must bring our individual circumstances before God with a yielded will that desires to know what he wants us to do.

May the God of hope fill you with all
joy and peace as you trust in him, so
that you may overflow with hope by the
power of the Holy Spirit.

—ROMANS 15:13

God is ready
to radically change things
because no obstacle
is too difficult for him.

TOTAL
TRANSFORMATION

At only twenty-nine years of age Maria's mom underwent major surgery for a brain tumor while she was pregnant. She did not survive but the tiny, two-and-a-half-pound baby did. Maria spent her first few months of life in the New York Foundling Hospital. Her dad then brought her home and hired a nanny. But when Maria was two and a half years old, he placed her in an expensive Roman Catholic boarding school.

Maria experienced great cruelty at the hands of the staff: punching was part of the physical abuse, the emotional abuse was horrific and then there was the sexual abuse. The staff carefully covered up the physical beatings, but an unannounced visit by Maria's dad brought everything to light and ended her stay at the boarding school.

It was a huge transition to go from the regimented life of the boarding school to the relative freedom of an apartment on the Lower West Side of Manhattan. Life on the streets was tough, but at least Maria was with her dad. In an effort to fit in, eleven-year-old Maria started sniffing airplane glue and

hanging out with the wrong crowd. At age twelve she began drinking, and by thirteen she was smoking pot.

By the time Maria was sixteen, her drug use had escalated to Quaaludes, "uppers," "downers" — anything that would take her away from reality. At eighteen she was shooting heroin and getting high on "acid," mescaline, and anything else she could lay her hands on. Her life became a series of near disasters as she survived a gas explosion, was hit by a car, attempted suicide once, and overdosed three times. One fateful day she came home to find her dad dead in the apartment.

Maria became a regular at disco clubs and after-hours nightspots in the city. She met and started living with a guy named Michael Durso, who seemed to be the answer to all her problems, and she fell deeply in love with him. But as time went on, the same old, empty feelings within her surfaced again. She could find nothing to satisfy them.

Michael and Maria went on a "honeymoon" to Mexico even though they weren't legally married. One evening Michael decided to go for a walk. Once again Maria was left alone to face her emptiness. For the first time in her life, she began to talk to God. "What kind of God are you?" she yelled. "Why am I alive and so empty and sad?"

Suddenly Maria heard a voice speaking to her heart! Gently it said, "Give me your life before it's too late." Although she didn't even know what those words meant, she decided to follow as best she could the new desires she was discovering.

Upon returning to New York, Maria realized she needed to call someone to find a church to visit. Her friend Barbara recommended a church in Brooklyn, and Maria eventually persuaded Michael to come with her. Although Michael took it as a joke, Maria knew she needed what she felt in that church. At the end of the service Maria walked forward to surrender her life to Christ.

God was obviously up to something very wonderful because Michael went forward with her!

The young, spaced-out couple who went to a simple gospel meeting were totally transformed from their previous lifestyle. Michael and Maria Durso now pastor Christ Tabernacle, one of the finest churches in New York City and God is blessing their ministry together as they share the life-changing power of Jesus Christ.

It is what God sees
behind the façade
and outward behavior
that determines the extent
of his blessing.

God showers people with rich and wonderful blessings. But how ungrateful and blind people are! They don't recognize these blessings as amazing miracles from God, so they don't admire them, give thanks for them, or act happy about them. However, if a clown can walk on a tightrope or train monkeys, people are ready to admire and praise him for it. The psalmist points out that the Lord's deeds are spectacular (Psalm 111:2), but these deeds are only appreciated in the eyes of God's faithful followers.

—MARTIN LUTHER
BY FAITH ALONE, DEC. 10

Praise be to the God and Father
of our Lord Jesus Christ! In his great
mercy he has given us new birth into a
living hope through the resurrection of
Jesus Christ from the dead, and into an
inheritance that can never perish, spoil
or fade—kept in heaven for you, who
through faith are shielded by God's power
until the coming of the salvation that
is ready to be revealed in the last time..

—1 PETER 1:3-5

*Because of the Lord's great love we
are not consumed,
for his compassions never fail.
They are new every morning:
great is your faithfulness.*

—LAMENTATIONS 3:22-23

CHANGE NO
MATTER WHAT

The Bible is always reminding us that
things don't have to remain the way they
are. If God is given the opportunity, his
blessings can bring about dramatic change
no matter what our circumstances are.
No negative situation, hostile environment,
or shortage of manpower is greater than
the power of Jesus Christ. He alone can
transform any one or any local congregation
into something more wonderful than we
could ever imagine.

I can do everything through Christ
who gives me strength.

—PHILIPPIANS 4:13

Blessings crown the head of the righteous.

—PROVERBS 10:6

May God himself, the God of peace,
sanctify you through and through.
May your whole spirit, soul and body
be kept blameless at the coming of our
Lord Jesus Christ. The one who calls you
is faithful and he will do it.

—1 THESSALONIANS 5:23–24

MAY THE ETERNAL GOD BLESS AND
KEEP US, GUARD OUR BODIES, SAVE
OUR SOULS, DIRECT OUR
THOUGHTS, AND BRING US SAFE TO
THE HEAVENLY COUNTRY, OUR
ETERNAL HOME, WHERE FATHER,
SON AND HOLY SPIRIT EVER REIGN,
ONE GOD FOR EVER AND EVER.

*Let us remember that
experiencing God's blessing
doesn't make us less
of a target for the devil.
In fact, it draws
his special attention.
But God is able to give
us the victory over
every satanic assault.*

LIVE IN VICTORY

Steven was born in New York City into a typical, middle-class home. His dad was a longshoreman, and his mom stayed at home to raise the children. It was a traditional Catholic home but eventually his parents divorced, ending the relatively normal and happy life Steven had enjoyed.

Steven's mother remarried and his new step-father was a hard man who seemed to have little patience. He routinely beat Steven, called him names, and threatened to send him away. When he was eleven, Steven had his first encounter with pornography when his brother showed him a lewd magazine. This planted a deadly seed that would yield much horrible fruit during the years to come.

"At seventeen," Steven says, "I decided to join the army. It seemed like I was always getting into trouble, and I barely made it through basic training. In the army I was exposed to more pornography and started going to strip clubs. Then I had my first sexual encounter with a prostitute. I had always been shy with girls, but now pornography, prostitutes, and strip clubs became an escape for me. I found acceptance there, and it seemed like someone actually showed affection to me."

At eighteen, Steven was kicked out of the army. For the next six years he moved about, while working as a bartender. He became more engrossed in pornography and sexual promiscuity. He took a job as a merchant seaman and traveled all over the world. Eventually Steven ended up back in Brooklyn, where he couldn't help but notice a change in the life of one of his friends.

"Paul shared with me about the love of Jesus," Steven recalls. "The change in him was so radical and obvious that, simply out of curiosity, I finally agreed to go to church with him. During the service, a simple gospel message was preached. The speaker said that God has a plan for every person and that to reject Jesus Christ was to choose hell over heaven and death over life. I knew my life was twisted and wrong, so on that Sunday morning, I put my faith in Jesus Christ as Savior."

Steven soon began attending the Brooklyn Tabernacle, where he served as an usher and in other ministries. God had changed his life, but the battle for his soul was far from over.

He began to struggle once again with lustful passions. During the next few years, Steven's spiritual life went up and down like a yo-yo. Victory lasted for a few weeks or months, followed by a fall back into the pit. Discouragement and fatigue set in, so Steven tried to run away. He took a job as a merchant seaman again and ended up on a cargo ship seven thousand miles away in the Persian Gulf.

"One day, as I walked out on the deck I ran into a foulmouthed merchant seaman who told me about Jesus! Immediately a deep conviction settled over my heart. I couldn't shake it off. I begged God to leave me alone, but the Lord did not abandon me. Instead, he reminded me of his love and mercy and kept reaching out to me in tenderness and compassion."

Steven returned to Brooklyn and began to learn how to live in victory. Instead of depending on his own strength or personal resolve, he yielded his problems and his life wholly to the Lord. Today Steven is one of the most spiritually minded men in our church. He is no longer addicted to pornography, and God's hand is upon him.

To live under the blessing of heaven is to always be running toward God with our guilt and not away from him (as if we could ever hide from him anyway). As we renounce our sin and turn from it, we give it up with full confidence that God will act in accordance with his Word. He will forgive freely. He will cleanse us from every stain of sin. He will help us because of his great love.

God has a wonderful plan for all his people. But he doesn't have to tell us much about it if he chooses not to. All he asks is that we take his hand and walk along in faith. He will show us soon enough what should be done.

Prayer is the avenue
God uses to come and
bless his people.

The Lord Jesus Christ be near to
defend thee,
  within thee to refresh thee,
  around thee to preserve thee,
  before thee to guide thee,
  behind thee to justify thee,
  above thee to bless thee;
who liveth and reigneth
with the Father and the Holy Spirit,
God for evermore.

God has a wonderful plan for all his people.

But he doesn't have to tell us much about it if

he chooses not to. All he asks is that we take

his hand and walk along in faith. He will

show us soon enough what should be done.

To live under the blessing of heaven is to always be running toward God with our guilt and not away from him (as if we could ever hide from him anyway). As we renounce our sin and turn from it, we give it up with full confidence that God will act in accordance with his Word. He will forgive freely. He will cleanse us from every stain of sin. He will help us because of his great love.

The Lord bless you
and keep you;
the Lord make his face shine upon you
and be gracious to you;
the Lord turn his face toward you
and give you peace.

—NUMBERS 6:24–26

At Inspirio we love to hear from you—
your stories, your feedback,
and your product ideas.
Please send your comments to us
by way of e-mail at
icares@zondervan.com
or to the address below:

inspirio™

Attn: Inspirio Cares
5300 Patterson Avenue SE
Grand Rapids, MI 49530

If you would like further information
about Inspirio and the products we
create please visit us at:
www.inspiriogifts.com

Thank you and God Bless!

SOURCES:

Appleton, George. *The Oxford Book of Prayer*. Oxford University Press, 1995.

Arnold, Duane W. H. *Prayers of Martyrs*. Zondervan, 1991.

Cymbala, Jim with Dean Merrill. *Fresh Faith*. Zondervan, 1999;
    Fresh Power. Zondervan, 2001; *Fresh Wind, Fresh Fire*. Zondervan, 1997.

Cymbala, Jim with Stephen Sorenson. *The Life God Blesses*. Zondervan, 2001.
    The Church God Blesses. Zondervan, 2002.

Luther, Martin. *By Faith Alone*. World Publishing, 1998.